The Sistine Chapel Ceiling by Michelangelo

A Quick Guide

Paul den Arend

Book design and production by VandiDesign
Editing by Paul den Arend

Published by: VandiDesign, Meerweg 112 9752 JL Haren, The Netherlands

CONTENTS

Paul den Arend

1 INTRODUCTION

The Sistine Chapel ceiling is one of the most beautiful and important artworks ever created. Even though Michelangelo considered himself a sculptor, he managed to paint an enormous influential work. Today, more people than ever flock to the Sistine Chapel to see it. A visit to Rome or Italy is not complete without it.

Most people just look at the painting and are struck by its beauty. To truly appreciate this work however, you have to know a little bit about it. If you know why this work was so influential and why we still today stand in line for many hours to go and see it, you will appreciate this monumental work even more.

Michelangelo did not just paint a few scenes from the bible and that was it. There is a story behind every fresco inside the Sistine Chapel and this book will tell you all these stories and, hopefully, make you enjoy the Sistine Chapel even more, whether you just look at it from pictures or go see it in real life.

2 THE SISTINE CHAPEL

The name Sistine Chapel comes from the Pope who commissioned the Chapel, Pope Sixtus IV of the Della Rovere family. The chapel was designed by Baccio Pontelli and built under the supervision of Giovannino de Dolci between 1473 and 1481. Sixtus built the chapel for different reasons. He wanted a chapel where he could attend mass in private. The Pope did not like to attend mass in Saint Peters, where everybody could see him. Besides that, the Chapel also has a clear defensive function. If you look at it from the outside it looks just like a fort.

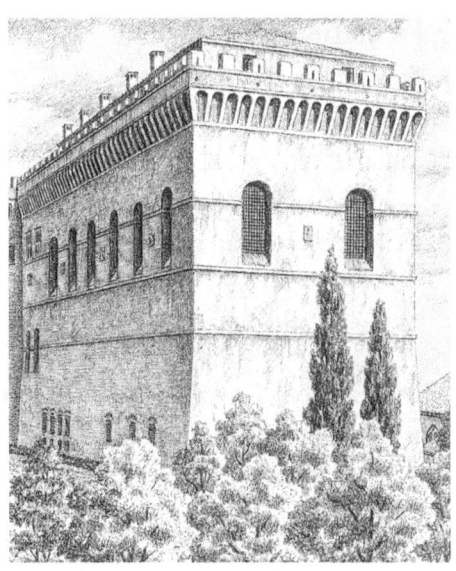

It is 22 meters high and also served as a fortress. It's outside is not decorated much, as was the custom in this time. There is no exterior façade. The building consists of three stories. The ground floor has very small windows and an exit to a courtyard. The first floor holds the actual Sistine Chapel. The vault of the chapel rises 20,7 meters high (68ft). Above the vault is another level, with guardrooms.

Another reason to build the chapel was that a place was needed to hold the conclave, the ceremony in which a new Pope is selected. The first mass in the Sistine Chapel was celebrated on 15 August 1483, the Feast of the Assumption, at which ceremony the chapel was consecrated and dedicated to the Virgin Mary.

After the chapel was finished, the ceiling was painted in blue, with gold starts. So the ceiling of the chapel looked nothing like how it looks now, with Michelangelo's beautiful fresco.

Then, Sixtus had the side walls painted by the most famous artists of his time. Painters like Botticelli, famous for painting the birth of Venus, worked in the chapel, but also artists like Perugino from Umbria and Ghirlandaio, who later became Michelangelo's teacher. All these frescoes were considered masterpieces. The artists were just very unlucky that decades later Michelangelo painted one of the most important works in western art on the ceiling of the chapel. So nowadays nobody looks at their frescoes, which is too bad, because they too are masterpieces in their own right.

It is possible that Perugino was supervising the whole project. Some say the fact that Florence's best painters did this work, was because of a reconciliation between Lorenzo de' Medici, the ruler of Florence and Sixtus, who had been at odds. The Florentines started working in 1481.

On one side we have can see scenes from the life of Jesus and the other side scenes from the life of Moses. Above these they painted the first 24 Popes of the Church. The reason that the life of Jesus is painted and the life of Moses on the other side is because the Church wanted to draw a parallel between the old testament and the new testament. It wanted to show the continuity between the two.

Let's look a bit more at these frescos on the side walls. The southern wall is decorated with frescos from the life of Moses. Starting from the altar, you first see Moses leaving to Egypt, by Pietro Perugino.

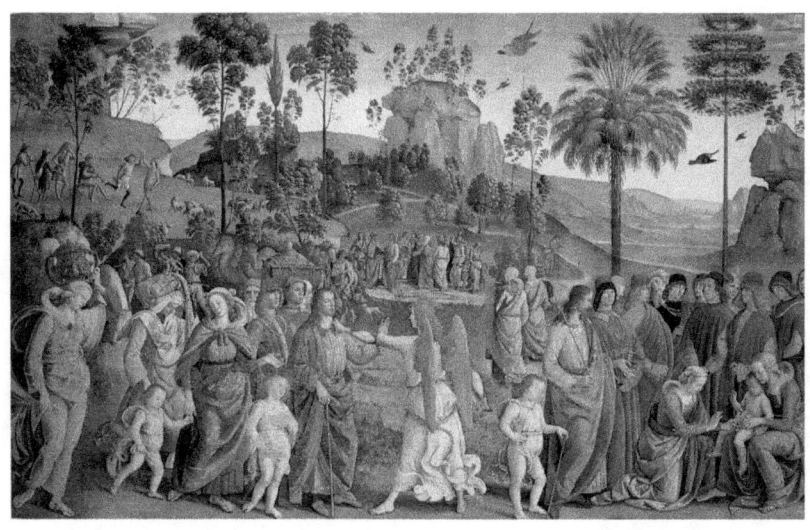

This fresco shows Moses leaving to Egypt, after he had been exiled from Midian. In all the frescos, Moses is recognizable by his yellow and green robes. Moses is depicted multiple times in this one fresco. This was very common in this time and comes from medieval painting. In the middle you can see an angel asking Moses to circumcise his son as a sign of the alliance between God and the Israelites. On the right in the fresco you can see the circumcision take place.

The next fresco depicts the trials of Moses and was painted by Sandro Botticelli.

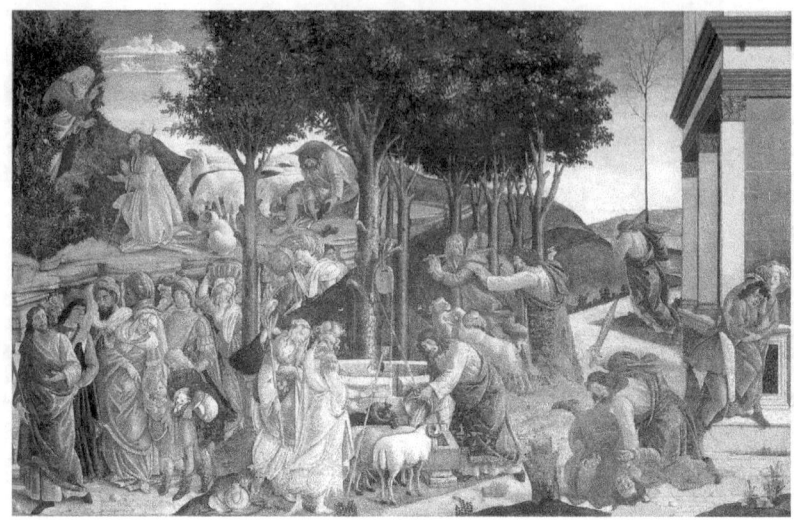

This fresco shows several episodes from when Moses was young, as written in exodus. On the right you can see Moses killing the Egyptian who had harassed a Hebrew, and then fleeing to the desert. In the scene in the middle, you can see Moses fighting the shepherds who refused to let Jethro's daughters let their cattle drink water. After Moses wins, he takes water for them (including his future wife, who is one of the daughters). In the upper left corner, you can see Moses removing his shoes as he receives the task from God to return to Egypt and free his people. In the lower left corner, you can see Moses leading the Jews to the promised land.

In detail of the work, you can clearly see that is was Botticelli who painted this work. Botticelli is most famous for the way he depicted women. They often had beautiful faces and blond hair. Maybe you know his painting 'The birth of Venus'. Look at this detail from the fresco in the Sistine Chapel:

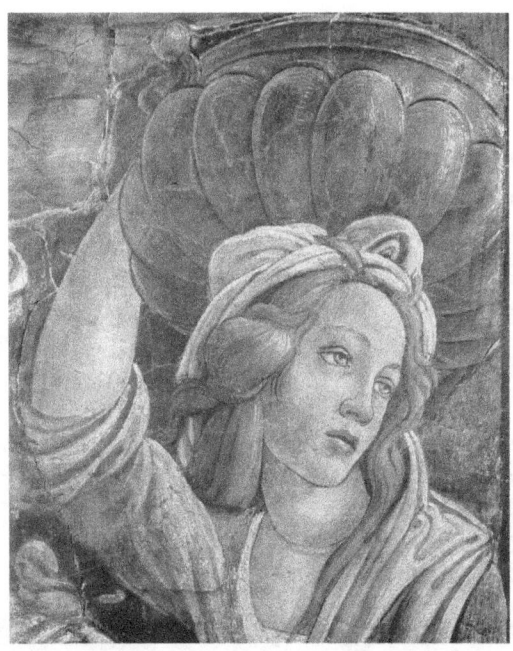

The next fresco is called The crossing of the red sea. It is often attributed to Domenico Ghirlandaio, but some art historians don't agree and believe it was painted by Cosimo Rosselli or Biagio d'Antonio.

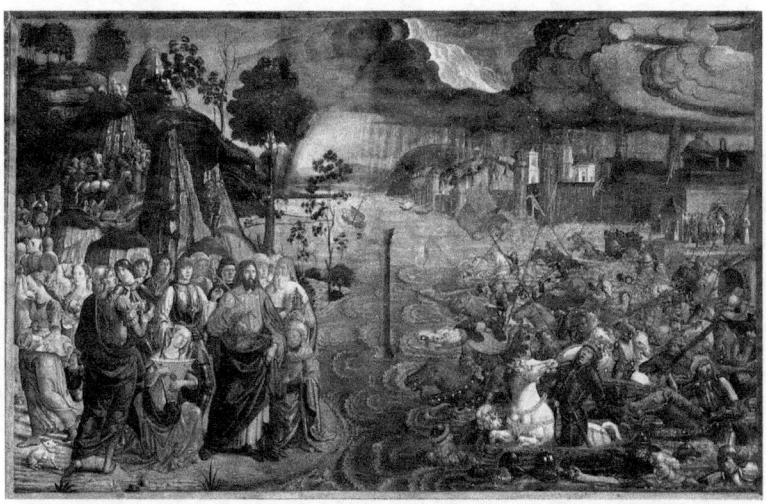

This scene shows different episodes at the same time, just as the other fresco's. In the right background, Moses is asking the Pharaoh to free the Israelites. The most impressive scene is the Egyptian soldiers drowning in the red sea on the right. They are drowning in full battle costume, being led by the Pharaoh, who lets out a big scream before drowning. On the left, Moses is looking at the drowning Egyptians with his Israelites.

The next fresco is by Cosimo Rosselli, who may or may not have also painted the fresco above. This one is called Descent from Mount Sinai.

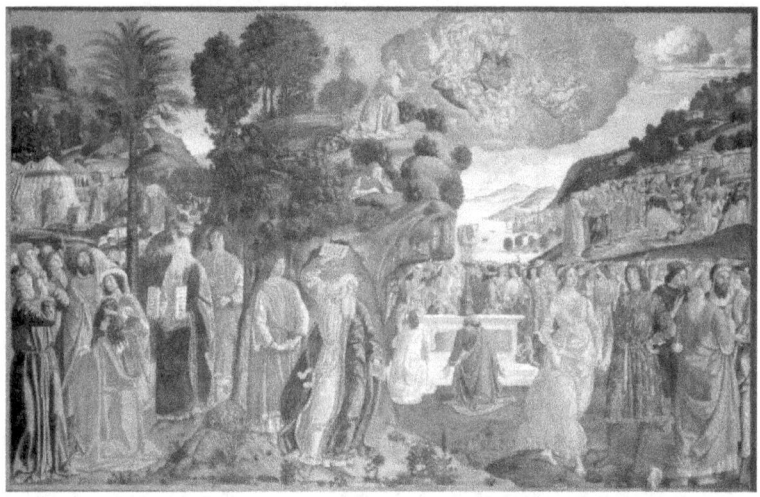

In the upper part, Moses is kneeling, with a sleeping Joshua. He receives the tables of the law by God, who appears from the cloud on the right. On the left in front you can see Moses bringing the law to the Israelites. In the background you can see them adoring the golden calf, led by Aaron. Right in the middle, we can see an angry Moses breaking the tables of the law in anger on the floor.

Next to this fresco, you can see the Punishment of the Rebels, by Sandro Botticelli.

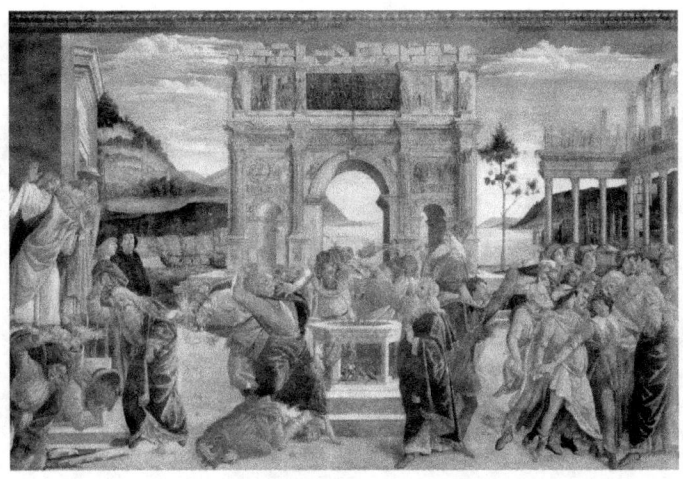

Again, three episodes are depicted. They all concern a rebellion by the Israelites against Moses and Aaron. The life of the Israelites had become very hard on the road from Egypt. On the right the rebels attempt to stone Moses. Joshua is trying to protect Moses from the stoning, by putting himself between his father and the rebels. In the center scene, the rebels are driven out by Moses and on the right, the main rebels disappear in a hole in the earth.

The last fresco depicts the Testament and Death of Moses. It is painted by Luca Signorelli and Bartolomeo della Gatta. The fresco shows the last episode in Moses' life.

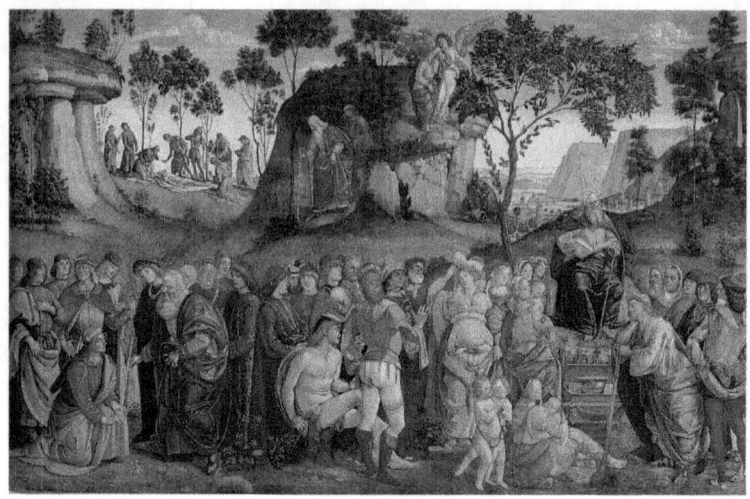

In the background, Moses receives the baton of command by an angel, which gives him the right to finally lead his people to the promised land. Up in the middle, Moses descends from a mountain with the baton in his hand. In the foreground, on the right, Moses, who is 120 years old now, is talking to the crowd. He holds the baton. At his feet is the Ark of the Covenant. On the left is the appointment of Joshua as Moses' successor.

On the northern wall, scenes from the life of Jesus are depicted.

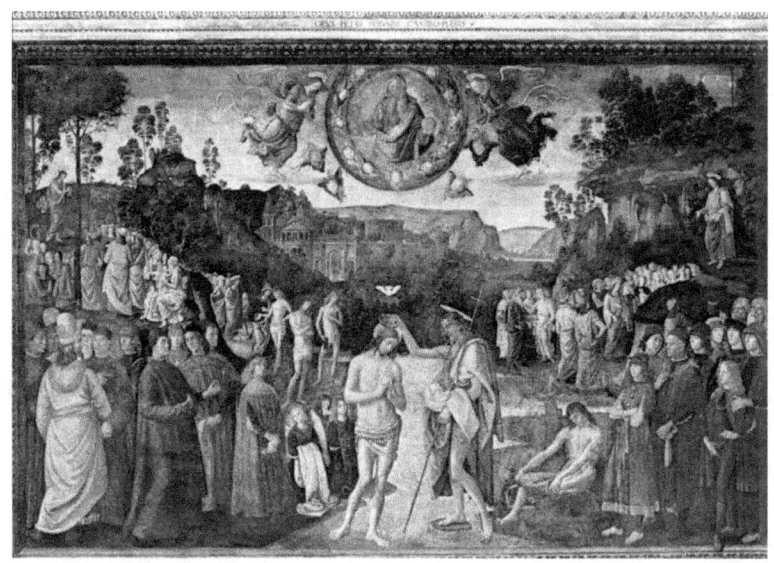

The first depicts the Baptism of Christ by Perugino. In the middle, Jesus is baptized by John the Baptist. The landscape includes a symbolic view of Rome, recognizable by a triumphal arch, the Colosseum and the Pantheon. At the sides you can see John the Baptist and Jesus preaching to a crowd. John is standing all the way on the left and Jesus all the way on the right.

The next scene depicts the Temptation of Christ and was painted by Botticelli.

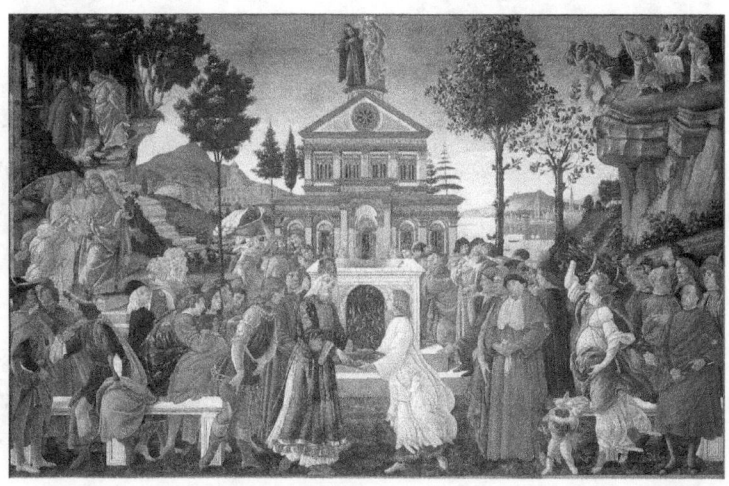

The main episodes in this fresco take place in the upper part. On the left upper part, you can see Jesus, who has been fasting, being tempted by the devil to turn stones into bread. In the middle, Jesus stands on top of the temple in Jerusalem. The devil says Jesus should throw himself down, to test God's promise to protect him. On the right, you can see the devil, who has taken Jesus to a mountain top. He promises Jesus the power over the earth if he bows down to him. Jesus sends the devil away.

In the foreground, you can see a man, who has been healed from leprosy by Jesus, present himself at the temple so he may be proclaimed clean.

In the next fresco, you can see the Vocation of the Apostles.

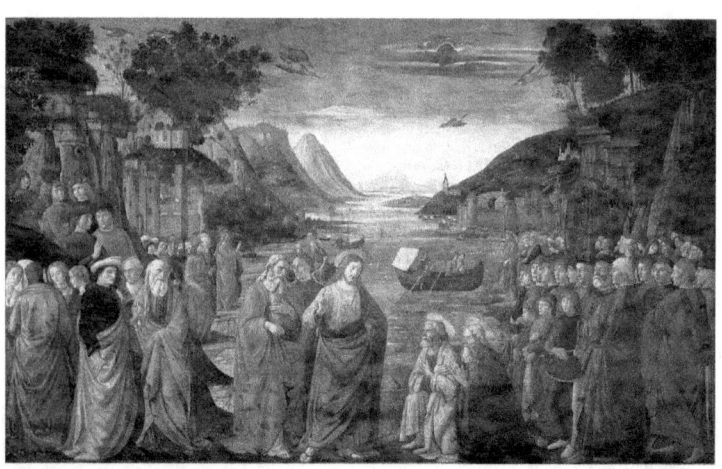

This was painted by Domenico Ghirlandaio, most famous for being a teacher to Michelangelo and the frescos in the Tornabuoni Chapel in the Santa Maria Novella in Florence. This scene shows fishermen Andrew and Peter, who are on their knees, as they are being called by Jesus.

The next scene depicts the Sermon on the Mount and it is painted by Cosimo Rosselli. After this, you can see the Delivery of the Keys by Perugino.

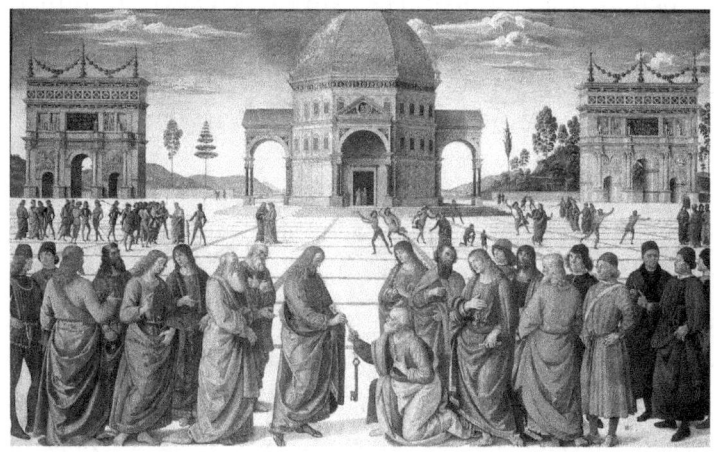

This scene is a reference to Matthew 16 in which the keys of the kingdom of heaven are given to Saint Peter. This is a very important scene for the Papacy. Jesus hands over his authority to forgive and spread the word of God to Saint Peter. The Popes consider themselves direct successors to Saint Peter, who is considered the first Pope.

The final scene is by Cosimo Rosselli again and represents the Last Supper.

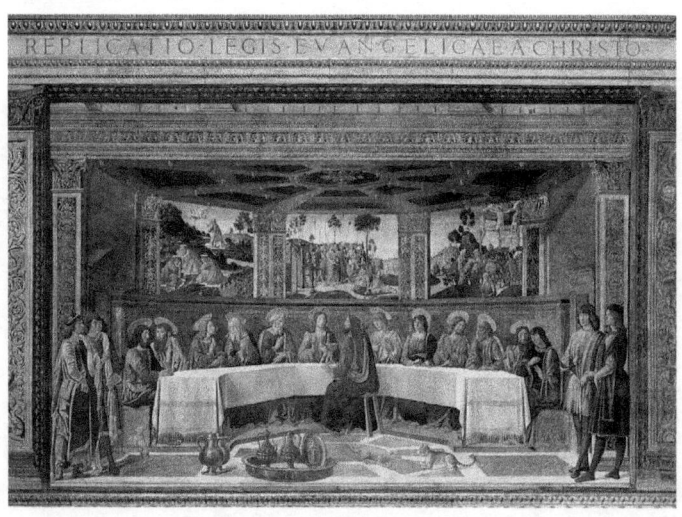

Judas, as usual, is depicted on his side and from behind. Can you see the fighting cat and dog? They are elements which further stress Judas' negative connotation. The scene shows the moment immediately after Jesus' annunciation he will be betrayed by one of the apostles. The apostles are shocked and raise their hands as they discus.

Sixtus IV was a typical Pope of the renaissance. So when he became Pope he made sure he made sure he advanced his family as well as he could. Even nowadays in Italy if you need a job you need to have an uncle somewhere who can help you. This is called nepotism, from the Italian word *nipote*, which means nephew. So when Sixtus became Pope he made sure that all his nephews got good jobs.

3 JULIUS II

One of Sixtus IV favorite nephews was Giuliano della Rovere. Immediately when he became Pope Sixtus made him a bishop and cardinal at age 28. At one point he held no less than 28 bishoprics. His ability and personality soon gave him an enormous influence over the college of cardinals, even after the death of his uncle. Then his archenemy was elected Pope. Cardinal Rodrigo Borgia from Spain became Pope Alexander VI. Giuliano accused him of bribing the cardinals to elect him and fled to France, where he convinced King Charles VIII to invade Italy to conquer the kingdom of Naples and depose the Pope. This did not work out as well as Giuliano intended, but after the death of Alexander and a short lived pontificate of Pius III, Giuliano managed to be elected Pope. He did this the same way Rodrigo Borgia had managed to secure the papacy: bribery. Some cardinals were offered money, some nice positions and in 1503 he was elected Pope. He took the name of Julius II.

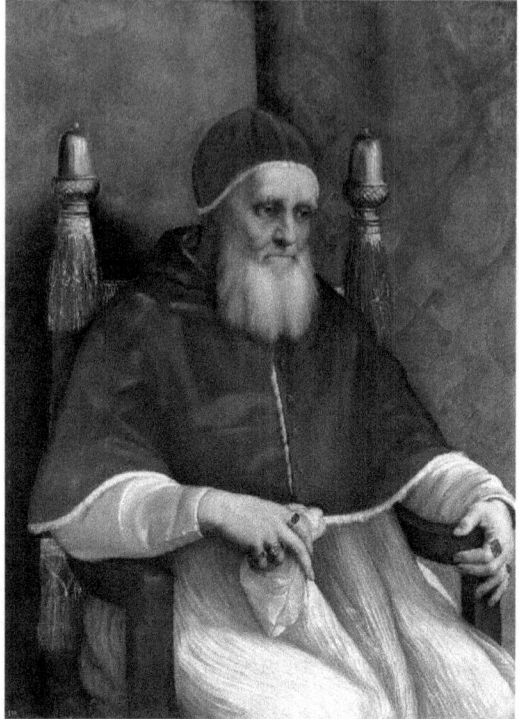

Figure 1 Julius II - Raphael

The names of these renaissance popes already tell you something about them. They are called Alexander, Julius and Leo. These are not very Christian names. Alexander of course refers to Alexander the great, Julius to Caesar.

The papacy of Julius was very important. He was called the warrior Pope. He liked to actually lead his troops into battle, something no other Pope had done before him. He re-conquered the Papal States and made sure they were firmly under his control. They say he preferred the smell of gunpowder to the smell of incense.

Besides all these activities on the battlefield Julius was very interested in the arts. He got some of the best artists and architects to Rome to work for him. He got the young Michelangelo to work for him on a tomb. This tomb was to be enormous and was meant to be put in in Saint Peters.

But then the Pope got a better idea. He decided, in order to be really remembered well, he had to start rebuilding Saint Peters basilica. In Julius' time the basilica was old and slowly falling apart. Once when alexander VI was holding mass a piece of the ceiling came down, which many people saw as an omen. The old basilica was commissioned by emperor Constantine at the beginning of the 4th century. Julius decided to rebuild it. He got one of the most famous architects of his time to Rome to work for him. His name was Donato Bramante.

4 THE CEILING

After this the Pope diverted all his time and marble to the project of the new church and the Pope lost interest in Michelangelo's work on his tomb. Instead he thought it would be a good idea to get Michelangelo to paint the ceiling of his uncle's chapel, the Sistine chapel. Michelangelo was very reluctant to take this commission, because he did not consider himself a painter. He thought of himself mainly as a sculptor. In fact, he was so angry that when the Pope was not paying attention he left for Florence and the Pope had to send people to get him back. He made Michelangelo sign the contract, which he stubbornly signed: the sculptor Michelangelo.

But, even though Michelangelo did not consider himself a painter and had never really painted fresco before, he managed to create one of the most important fresco paintings ever made. Michelangelo had the capacity to become extremely good at something in a very short period of time.

Why did the Pope have this strange idea to get his greatest sculptor to paint? Some say the idea came from the architect of the new Saint Peter, Bramante. He wanted to see Michelangelo fail, which would have been a logical outcome since fresco painting is a very difficult technique. Bramante hoped then to be able to convince the Pope to give the commission to one of his protégées, the young unknown Raphael from Urbino. This plan of course failed completely because of Michelangelo's genius.

The Pope wanted a complex ceiling with many different layers of meaning. Michelangelo gave him precisely that. Michelangelo decided to paint 9 scenes from the book of Genesis.

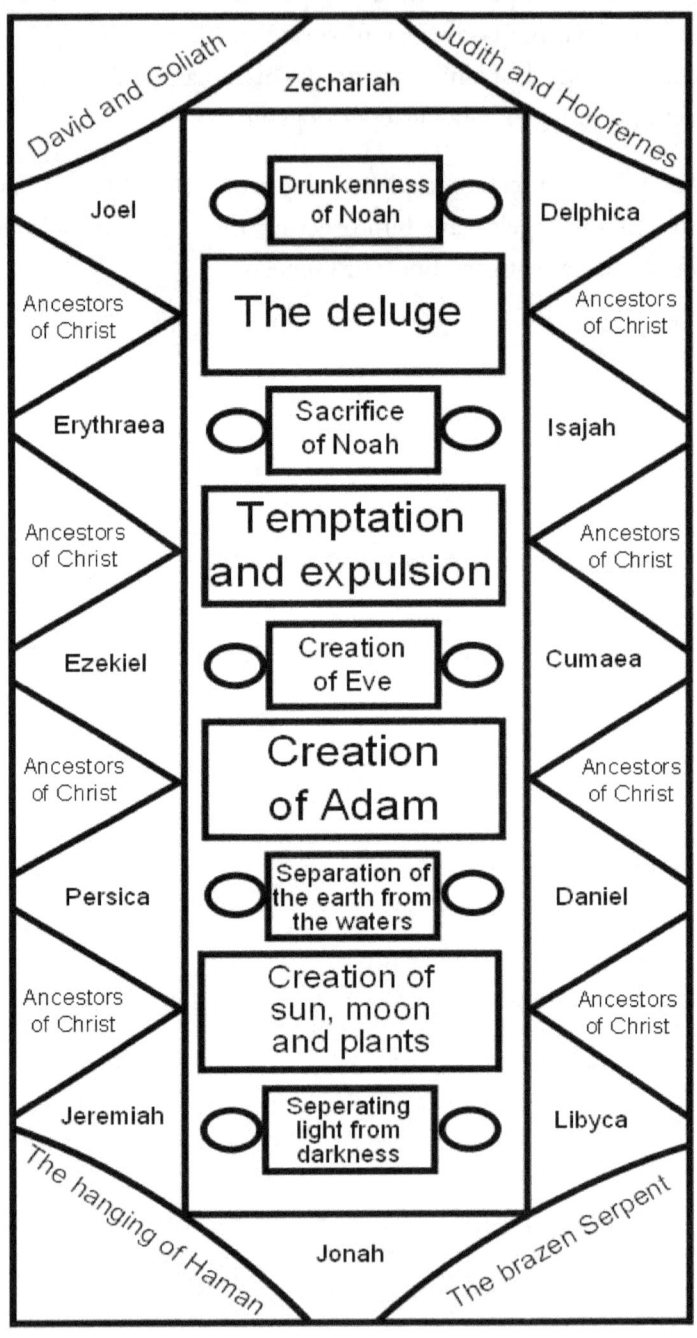

The four Pendentives

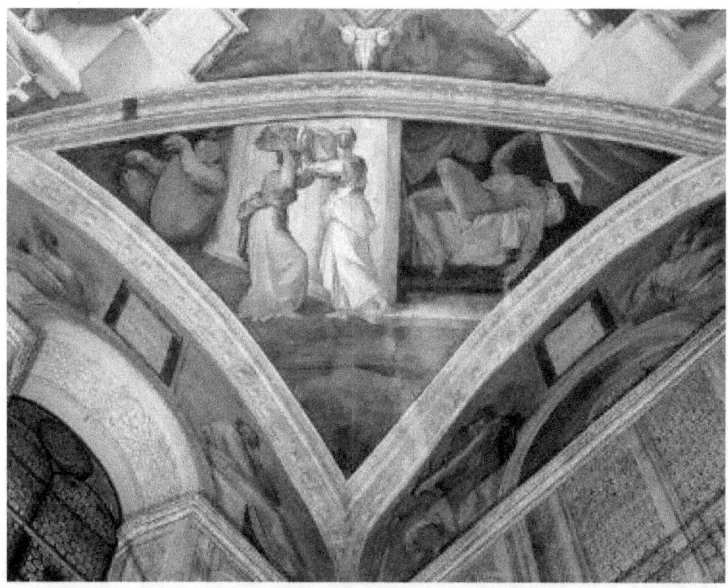

In the four pendentives we can see four miraculous salvations of the Jewish people by famous female heroines. You can see scenes from the stories of the brazen serpent, the punishment of Haman, David and Goliath and Judith and Holofernes.

The Niches

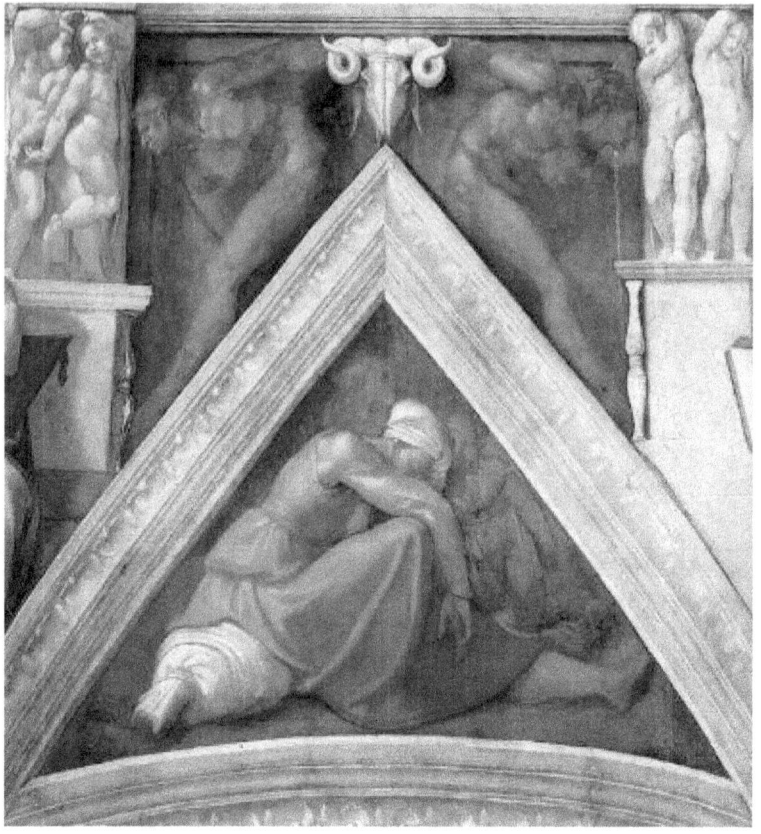

Within the niches you can see people sitting and lying down. These people symbolize the people that lived before Christ. They look bored and trapped in time. They are symbolically waiting for Christ to come and release them from the original sin

.

Prophets and Sibyls

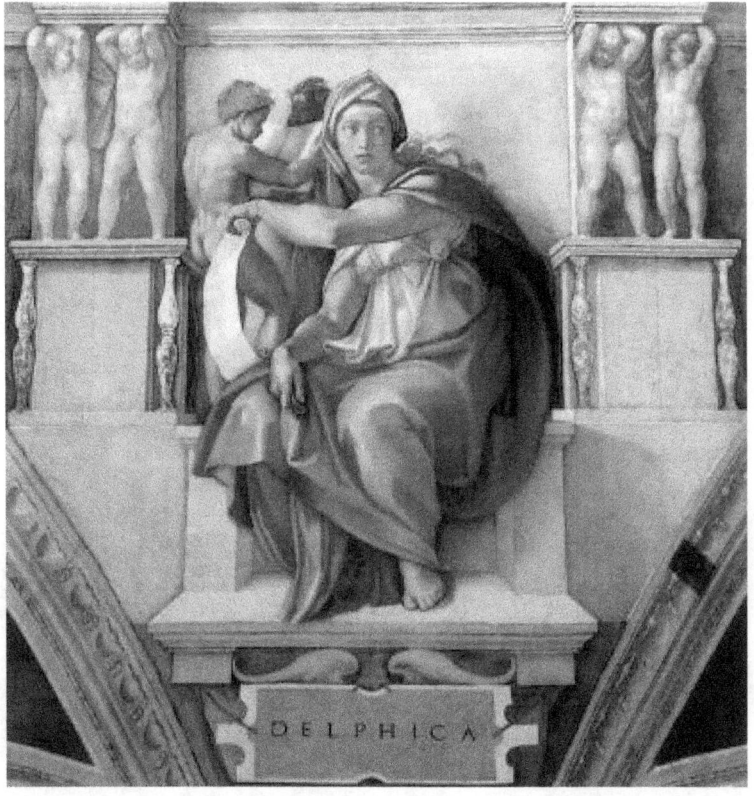

Then you can see big figures of prophets from the old testament and female sibyls, who are pagan prophetesses. These figures prophesize the coming of Christ. Why did he also paint pagan figures? In the renaissance people thought that even in roman and Greek times there were signs about the coming of Christ. The people just did not know how to interpret these signs.

Jonah

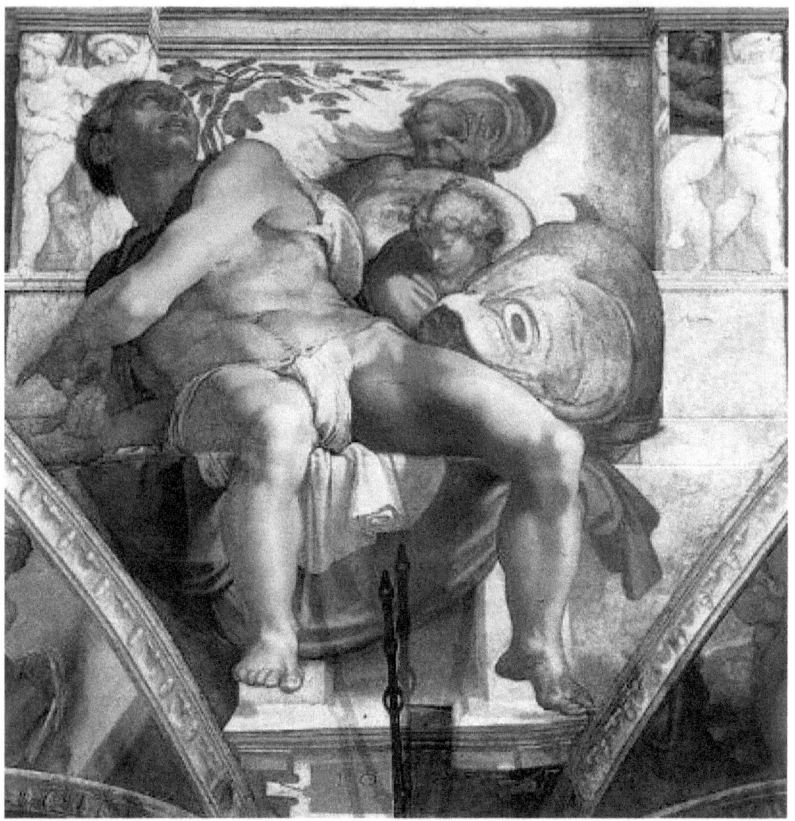

Jonah is also painted. He is a very big figure due to his importance and connection to Christ. Jonas stayed three days inside the whale, Lazarus was resurrected by Jesus after three days and of course also Jesus was resurrected after three days. So all these figures point to the coming of Christ. Christ is never painted but everything points to Him.

Ignudi

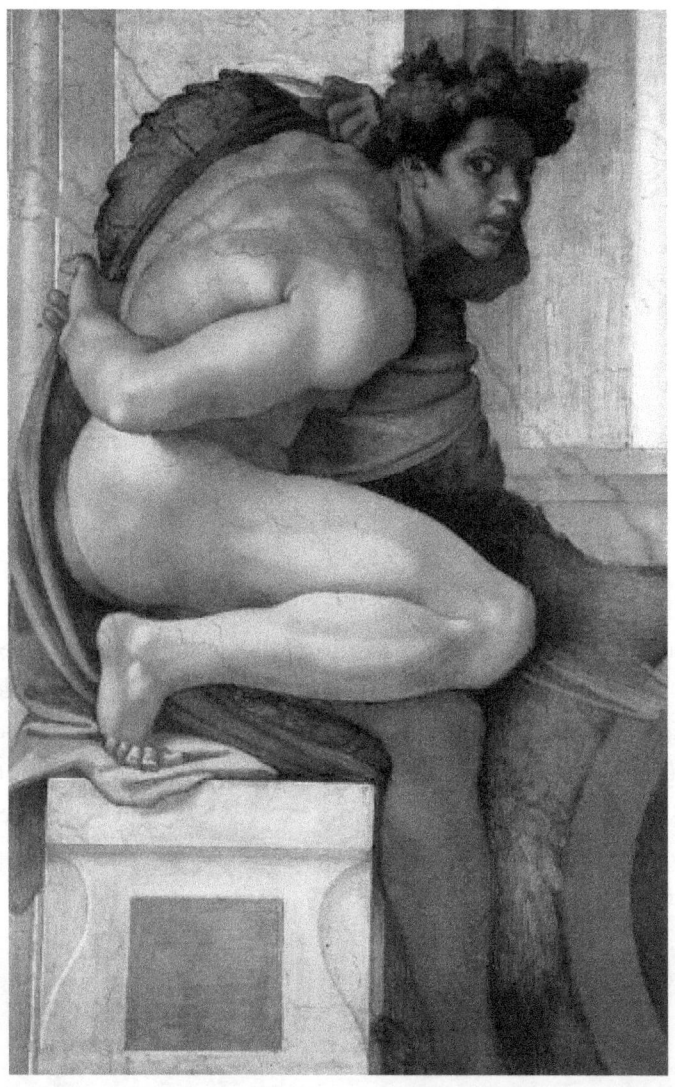

You can also see a lot of naked people. They are called ignudi, which basically is Italian for naked people. Do you remember the Torso Belvedere, the statue without head, arms and feet we saw before? All these naked figures are different interpretations of that statue. We can see Michelangelo imagining what the statue would have looked like.

5 NINE SCENES FROM GENESIS

The first three scenes that Michelangelo painted are scenes from the life of Noah. You can see he painted these scenes first. Why? Look at them. Look at the figures. What can you see when you compare these figures with the figures he painted later. These figures are much smaller. He painted these scenes, took down the scaffolding and looked up. He saw that the figures are too small to make a big impression. So for the next 6 scenes he painted the figures much bigger. And of course he was right, because those scenes are the scenes we all remember and by postcards and posters of, like the creation of man.

The Drunkenness of Noah

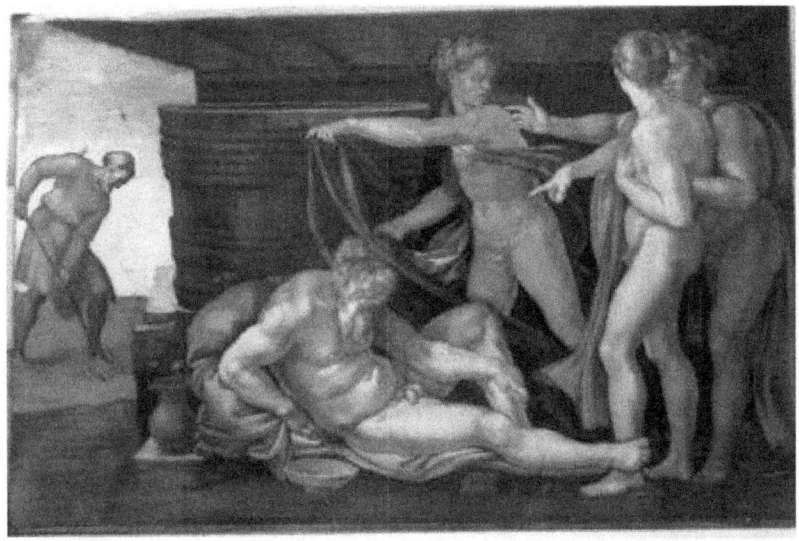

The first scene depicts the drunkenness of Noah. This is a story that takes place after the flood. We see him first working in the vineyard, and then, after making wine he gets drunk and passes out completely naked. Ham, his son goes inside his tent and sees his father naked. He then goes out and tells his brothers about it, who go into Noah's tent and cover him up without looking at him. When Noah wakes up, he then curses Noah's son Canaan, who becomes the ancestor of the enemies of Israel, the Canaanites. This is a complicated story and even biblical scholars are not quite sure what it means. Why Michelangelo painted this here I will tell you later.

The Flood

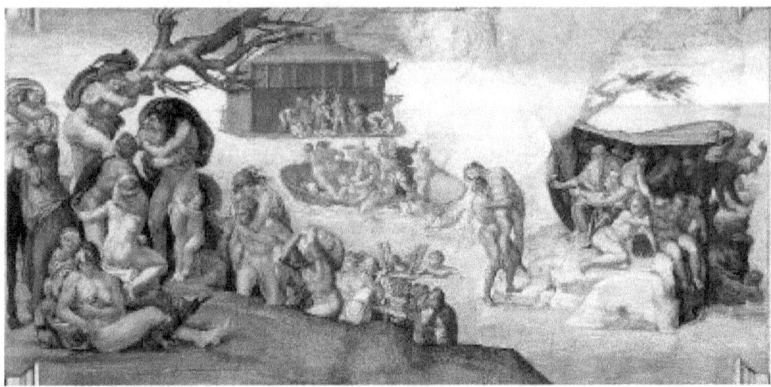

Then in the next scene we see the flood. It rained forty days and forty nights, because god wanted to rid the earth of the wicked people. Only Noah and his family was allowed to stay alive. We see the Ark Noah built and in the foreground the last humans who try to escape the flood by climbing the highest mountains.

The sacrifice of Noah

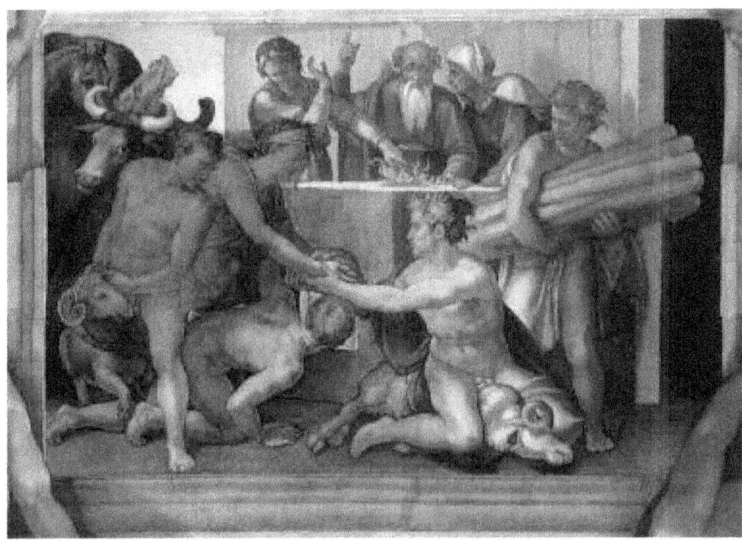

The next scene is The sacrifice of Noah. He built an altar and sacrificed a ram to God to thank Him for saving him from the flood. If you look closely you can see there is a part missing. The ceiling was damaged because of an explosion at Castel Sant'Angelo in 1797 when Napoleon invaded Rome.

Adam and Eve

The next cycle shows scenes from the life of Adam and Eve. As I said before, you can clearly notice the difference in style between the scenes of Noah and the rest. These figures are a lot bigger and are far more impressive. The scenes are not as complicated. This makes the compositions are a lot more striking. The creation of Adam, which is probably the most famous scene in the entire fresco painted in one day.

The creation of Man

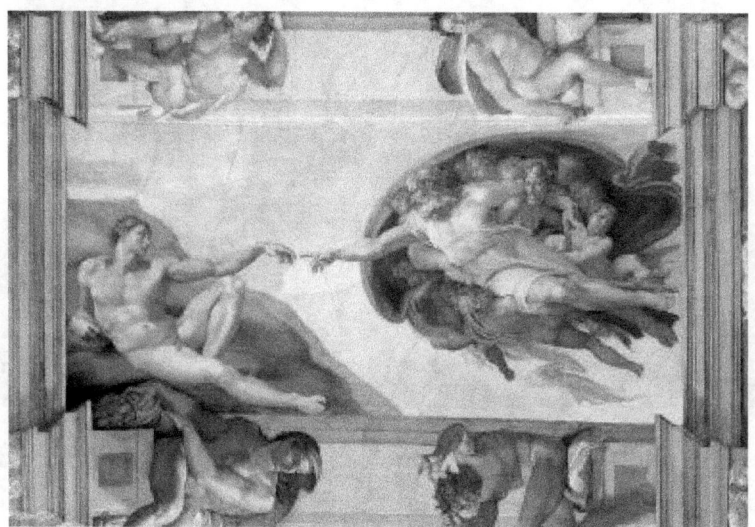

In this fresco we see God creating man with the touch of a finger. He puts life in him through a touch. This is a very original composition. This was never before painted like this.

Look at the shape behind God. What does this remind you of? A few years a neurologist wrote a famous essay about this form. He was convinced this form is a pretty accurate cross-section of a human brain. This is very well possible, because Michelangelo was one of the very few people in Europe who had studied corpses. He had gotten special permission to dissect dead bodies. So he would have known what a brain looks like. So the idea here is that all creation was already in God's brain when he created Adam. And you can see eve and other people behind god in his brain, waiting to be created.

The creation of Eve

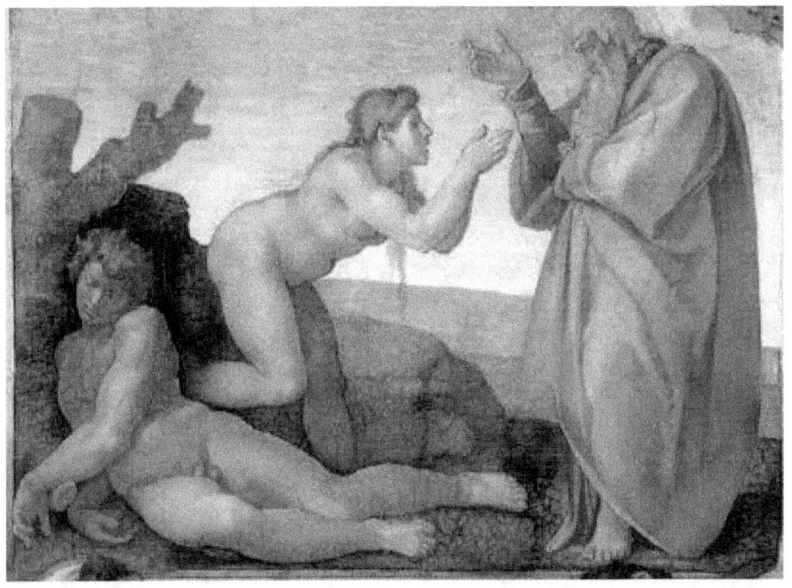

The next scene is the Creation of Eve. God decided that Adam needed a companion and therefore took a rib from him and created Eve out of this. We can see Eve thanking God for being created.

The expulsion from paradise

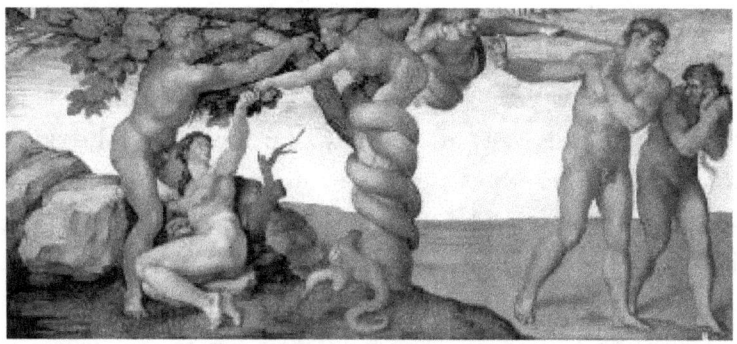

Then we see the story of the expulsion from paradise depicted, These are also a very famous scenes. We see two scenes divided by the tree of good and evil. On the left Adam and Eve are tempted by the snake to eat the forbidden fruit, which in this case is not an apple but a fig. Also the snake is a female figure. Both choose to eat the fruit. You can see Adam picking his own fruit and Eve accepting the fruit from the snake.

On the right side we see them both being cast away from paradise by an Angel. Can you see how Adam and Eve change? On the left they are young and beautiful but on the right they have aged, they try to cover their naked bodies, because they have learned shame. Look at their expressions. Now they have to suffer.

Now let's look at this fresco and compare this one to the ones made by the artists from a generation before Michelangelo. Look at the figures on the frescoes on the side walls and then to the figures in the fresco about the expulsion of paradise. Can you see a difference?

A big difference of course is that Michelangelo's figures are naked, but this is not the difference I am looking for. Look at the composition of the figures. Can you see the figures on the side-walls look like they are made from cardboard? They are very 2 dimensional. It looks like if you would blow, they would fall over. Now look back to Michelangelo's fresco. Can you see how three dimensional the figures are? Michelangelo's figures always have a lot of tension in them, which makes them look more alive. They are always positioned in a difficult position. Now what do you think of Michelangelo's landscapes? Can you see any? Compared to the painters on the side-walls his landscapes are really bad. Look at how beautiful the landscapes of Perugino and Botticelli are. Michelangelo was a sculptor and what he did is just paint the sculptures he had in his head. If you look at all the figures on the ceiling you can see that they all look like three dimensional sculptures. This is why we are still talking about Michelangelo. He really gave life to the figures in his paintings (and sculptures as well for that matter). His art was also of a very important influence on the style that came after him, the baroque.

The creation of the world

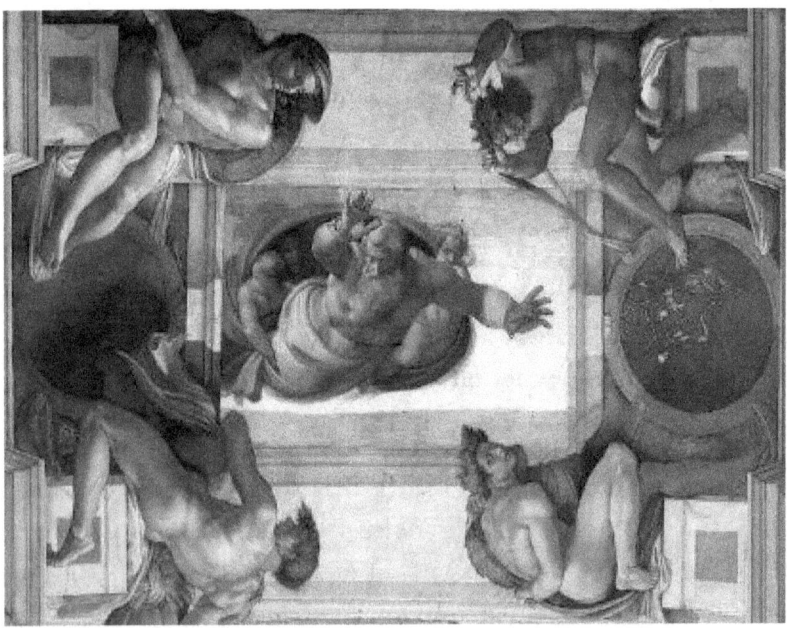

The next three scenes show God creating the world. First we see Him dividing the waters from the land and below that he is creating the sun and the moon. Here we see God turned around and creates the plants.

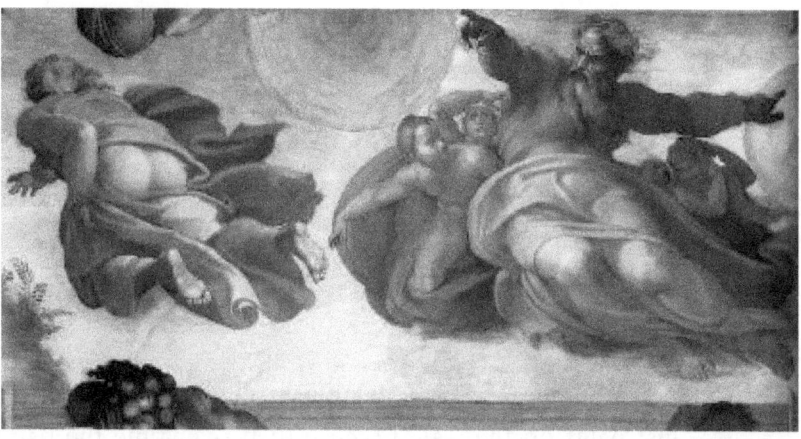

In the last scene we see him dividing light and darkness thus creating night and day.

The rest of the ceiling

Let me also point out these bronze people, they are waiting to be born. Michelangelo used the same cartoon; he just turned it over to save time.

The gold medallions were supposed to tell other stories from the old testament, but these were left unfinished because the gold was not available and the Pope could not wait any longer to celebrate mass.

6 FRESCO PAINTING

The technique of fresco painting is very difficult. You do not just paint on the wall, because then over time the paint will fall down. You have to paint on fresh plaster. The word fresco means fresh in Italian. Then when the plaster dries the paint is stuck inside. So you paint in the wall and not on the wall. This means every day the painter has to apply as much plaster as he is going to paint on that day. Michelangelo first would make life size sketches on paper and then put tiny holes in the lines of the drawing. He would then blow charcoal through the hole on the wet plaster. During the restoration it came to light that he stopped using this technique after a while and started painting directly on the ceiling. So you can see his technique improving. Very few painters were capable of painting directly on the plaster without making mistakes.

7 WHAT DOES IT ALL MEAN?

Now what is the general meaning of all these paintings? The general theme is the coming of Christ. Like I said before, everything points to Christ even if he is not depicted himself. But there are more meanings. Why did Michelangelo paint these exact 9 scenes from the old testament? This has to do with sin.

The main door of the chapel is not the small door you came in through. It is of course the big, closed door on the other side of the altar. If you would come in through this door and you would look up what would you see? You first see the drunkenness of Noah. So you will see sin.

Then the next scenes also have something to do with sin. God punishes humankind through a flood. Humans are expelled from paradise because they have sinned. But then as you walk forward and get closer to the altar who do you get closer to? Of course this is God, the main fresco above the altar is the beginning, which is God creating light and dark. So as you walk forward you get closer to god. Of course the altar also symbolizes God. So it is the human journey to go from sin to god.

8 THE WORK

Michelangelo started painting May 12 1508 and mass was given on October 31st 1512, so it took four years to paint the whole ceiling. Michelangelo worked 18 hours a day and ate and slept very little. He slept on the scaffolding he built and when he woke up he would continue working. After he finished he said he had difficulty straightening his neck and if he wanted to read a letter he had to hold it above his head. We have little sketches of Michelangelo where he draws himself painting. He was not lying on his back as many people believe but standing up straight, looking up and paint. A letter from Michelangelo: To Giovanni da Pistoia "When the Author Was Painting the Vault of the Sistine Chapel" — 1509

I've already grown a goiter from this torture,

hunched up here like a cat in Lombardy

(or anywhere else where the stagnant water's poison).

My stomach's squashed under my chin, my beard's

pointing at heaven, my brain's crushed in a casket,

my breast twists like a harpy's. My brush,

above me all the time, dribbles paint

so my face makes a fine floor for droppings!

My haunches are grinding into my guts,

my poor ass strains to work as a counterweight,

every gesture I make is blind and aimless.

My skin hangs loose below me, my spine's

all knotted from folding over itself.

I'm bent taut as a Syrian bow.

Because I'm stuck like this, my thoughts

are crazy, perfidious tripe:

anyone shoots badly through a crooked blowpipe.

My painting is dead.

Defend it for me, Giovanni, protect my honor.

I am not in the right place—I am not a painter.

9 THE LAST JUDGEMENT

After Michelangelo was finished he hoped never to paint again. He went on and created many more beautiful sculptures but after 24 years a new Pope decided he wanted Michelangelo to finish what he had started. It was Pope Paul III who became a very important patron of Michelangelo. Not only did he commission him to paint the last judgment in the Sistine chapel, he also convinced him that he would be a good architect. So he made him chief architect of Saint peters, made him design a new Capitoline Hill and gave him many more project.

Michelangelo was now in his sixties, He started painting the Last Judgment, the enormous fresco you see painted at the altar wall in 1535 and finished 1542. It took him six years to finish. two windows from the altar wall had to be closed and other frescos destroyed, including parts of Michelangelo's own work.

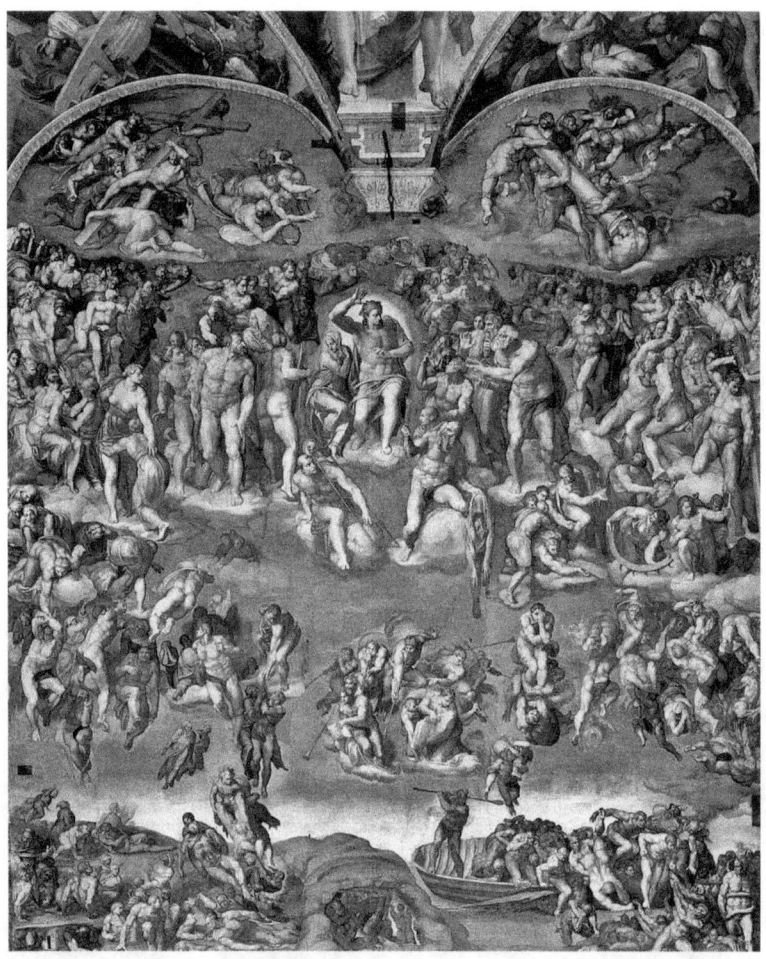

The tone of this work is very different from that of the ceiling. The ceiling is about the coming of the savior. This work is much darker. It is the last judgment.

Christ

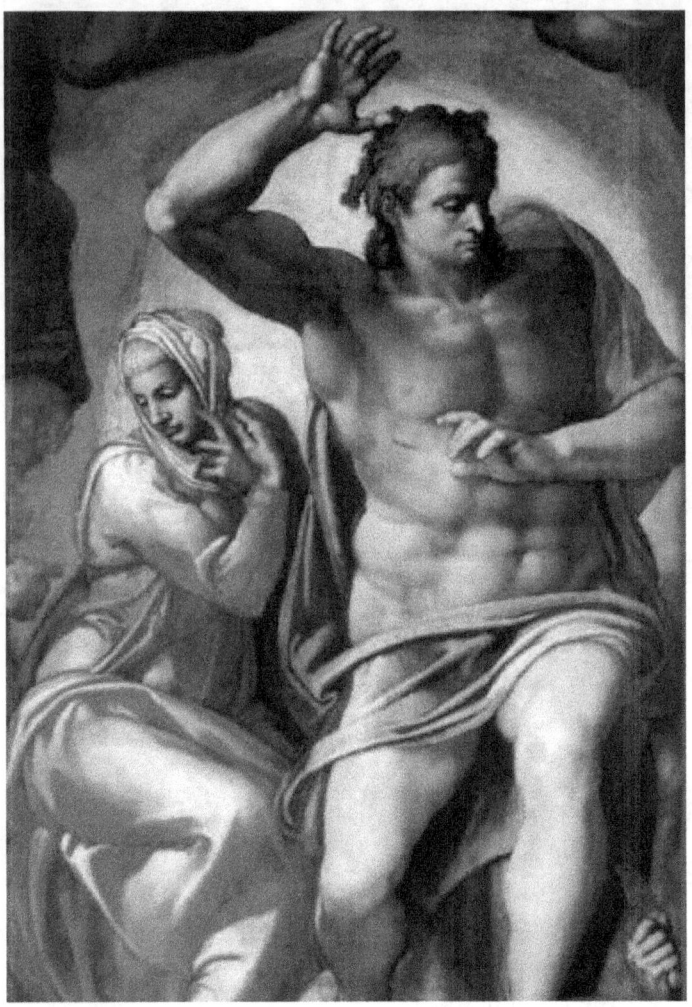

High in the middle of the fresco we see Christ. Now, does he look like the traditional Christ you see in other paintings? Not at all. He is beardless and very muscular. He looks almost like a classical god, which is not so strange to think, because Michelangelo used two statues we have seen earlier as a model for Christ. For his head he used the statue of the Apollo belvedere which we saw in the octagonal courtyard, and for his body he used the Belvedere Torso. He is a powerful figure. With one hand he raises the dead from their graves and with the other one he judges. He decides who goes to heaven and who goes to hell.

The Angels

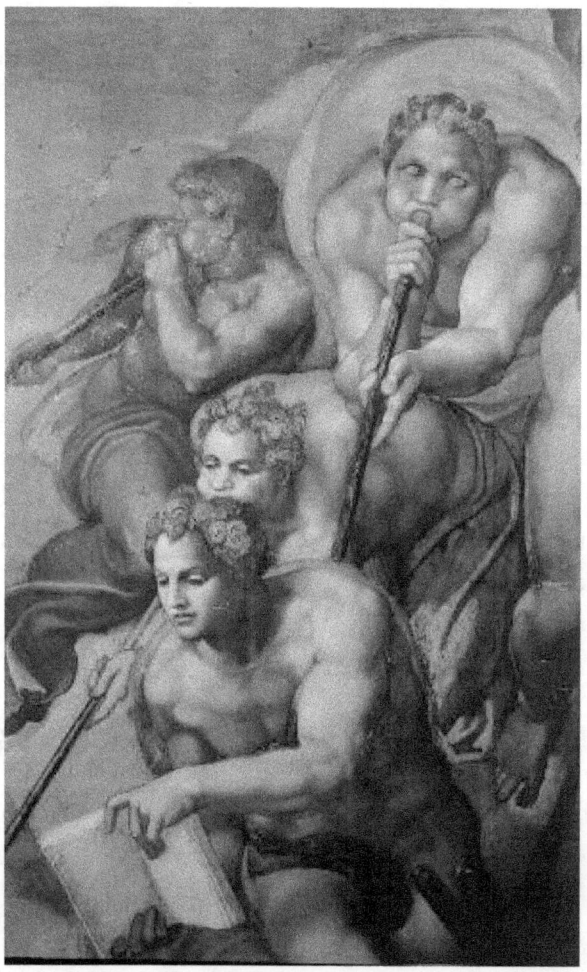

If you look below Christ you these wingless angels with trumpets. They awaken the dead. They carry two books. One book contains the list of the blessed souls and one of the damned. Can you guess which one is which? Of course the small book contains the list of the blessed. Only very few people will go to heaven, most will go to hell.

The fresco has a very dark subject. This has everything to do with the time it was painted in. 24 years had passed since Michelangelo painted the ceiling and the positive spirit of the renaissance had faded. In 1527 the troops of Emperor Charles V had sacked Rome and Michelangelo was there when it happened. It is said this was the worst sack of the city ever, including the ones by the barbarians after the fall of the west-roman empire. Priests were murdered, nuns were raped, artworks destroyed. The unfinished basilica of Saint Peters was used as a stable.

Also in 1517 another thing had happened. In Germany there was an Augustinian monk who absolutely did not like the way the Popes were behaving. Traveling monks were selling indulgences in Germany to fund the building of Saint Peter's and the many wars the popes were fighting. If you bought an indulgence you could secure your place in heaven according to the Pope. This monk started a protest and in 1517 he put 95 theses on the church door in Wittenberg where he lived at the time. His name of course was Martin Luther and he started the protestant revolution. The Catholic Church lost many believers in the northern parts of Europe.

So the message in the fresco is beware of what you do. You have to follow the right path, the catholic path or else you are going to go to hell. Next to Christ we can see Saint Peter. His face is a portrait of Pope Paul III. We also can see on the left side a figure who is pulled up to heaven by an angel using a rosary. Of course Luther had said that rosaries are useless, so this is a clear attack on Luther by Michelangelo.

Saints

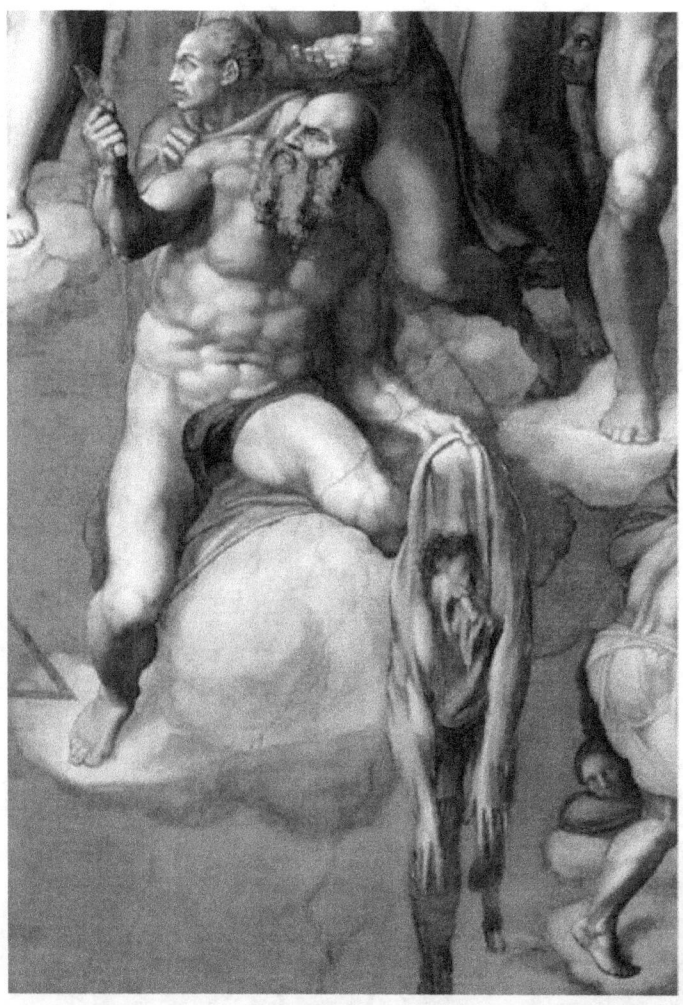

Around Christ we see many Saints. On the right side with the keys to heaven in his hand we can see Saint Peter. This is a portrait of Pope Paul III. On the right side below Christ we see Saint Bartholomew. He is holding his own skin in his handed because he was skinned alive. Now if you look at the skin it is not the same as Saint Bartholomew. It is actually a portrait of Michelangelo. He shows himself empty and tired because of all the work he had to do.

Left of Bartholomew we see Saint Lawrence. He is holding a grill in his hand because he was grilled alive. He was martyred during the reign of emperor Valerian. According to legend they grilled him alive and at a certain point Lawrence lifted himself up and said You can turn me over now, this side is done.

Above him you can see Saint Andrew with his back turned to us. He is recognizable by the cross he is holding which is shaped like an X.

Left of Andrew we see Saint John and to his right side you see Mary next to Christ. She turns her head, because she is sorry for the people that go to hell.

All these figures represent the most important Churches in Rome. Saint Peters, Santa Maria Maggiore, Saint John in Lateran etc

More Saints

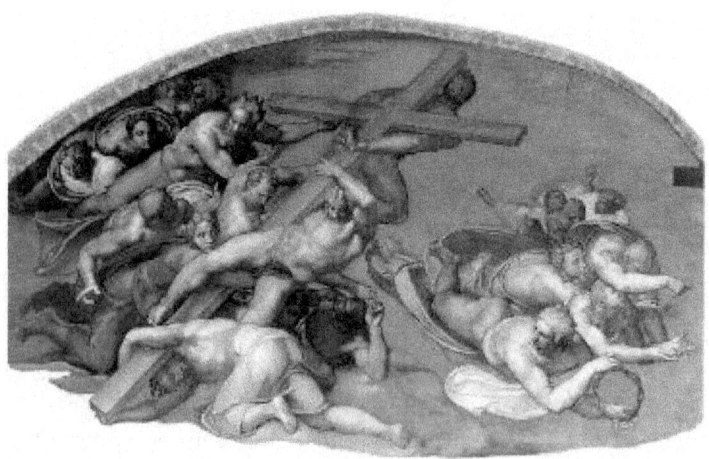

Above Christ you can see angels holding up his crown of thorns, the Cross and the pillar against which Christ was whipped.

Then on your right side you can see this group of saints. You can see Saint Sebastian all the way on the right, holding the arrows he was pierced with in his hand. Next to him is Saint Catherine of Alexandria, holding the wheel which she was tortured on. Now if you would go to the Capodimonte museum in Naples you could see a copy of this fresco done by an artist a few years after Michelangelo had finished. The amazing thing is that on this copy all these figures are naked. These were all dressed after Michelangelo had died and in the rest of the fresco many private parts were covered up, because later Popes thought the painting was indecent.

Hell

Then lastly on the right side just above the door we see hell. People are brought to Hell on a boat by Charon, a classical depiction of hell. In hell itself we see a man with ears like an ass and a snake around him. The snake bites him in a very unpleasant spot. This is a portrait of Biago de Cesena, who was the Pope's master of ceremonies. When he saw the fresco when Michelangelo was working on it he said it belonged in a brothel and not in a church. This, because there were so many naked pictures in the painting. Michelangelo heard this and painted him in Hell as Minos, the judge of the underworld. Of course Biago was furious and went to see the Pope to complain. But Paul III said that as Pope he just had power over heaven, but whatever happened in hell he could not influence. So Biago is still there.

The chapel was restored between 1981 to 1993, so it took 12 years to restore what one man painted in ten years. The company that paid for the restoration was Nippon, a Japanese TV network. They paid 100 million dollars. It took hundred experts to restore everything. What Nippon asked for in return was exclusive photography right of the Sistine chapel for 10 years. What the art historians amazed the most after the restoration was done were the colors of the chapel. It turned out Michelangelo had used much brighter colors than anybody had ever believed. Because of candle smoke the frescoes had become dark, but when they were restored people at first thought the restorers had repainted the ceiling.

10 THE SISTINE CHAPEL TODAY

The Sistine Chapel is still used today for ceremonies like the election of the Pope. This is called a conclave, which comes from the Latin Cum Clave, which means with key. The cardinals are locked inside the chapel. In earlier times this was to make them quickly choose a new Pope. In medieval times it would sometimes take years before a new Pope was elected, so at some point the cardinals were locked inside the chapel to make sure they would hurry up. During a conclave a little stove is put in the chapel and a chimney leads the smoke out. through the window. The cardinals write the name of their papal choice on a piece of paper and then votes are counted by three cardinals. Then the voting papers are burned. Before damp straw was added if no Pope was elected to turn the smoke black, but now they use chemicals. White smoke will appear from the chimney if the election is successful and nowadays also the bells will ring to make it absolutely clear.

There is a persistent legend the new Pope must be checked if he is male by feeling his testicles. This is an utter fabrication, which comes from the legend of Popess Joan, which is also a legend and nothing more.

Of course if a cardinal is elected he must first accept. After this he will go to a small room next to the Sistine chapel, which is called the crying room. Here he dresses himself in papal gowns. Three sizes are ready ever since John XXIII did not fit in his gowns. The new Pope is then taken to the balcony of Saint Peter's and is introduced by the Latin phrase: Annuntio vobis gaudium magnum: Habemus Papam, which means I announce to you a great joy, we have a Pope.

If you decide to visit the chapel, here are some essential tips:

• Make sure to book your tickets to the Vatican museums in advance on the official website of the Vatican. It's www.vatican.va. The lines to the museums can be much too long in the high season which runs from April until November. It's not fun spending hours in line and with an online ticket you can just enter through the special gate for advance bookers. You have to pay a bit more for the tickets, but it is really worth it.

• If you didn't book your ticket in advance, I would try to get in at lunch time, or even in the afternoon. Most guidebooks advise you to go early in the morning and that is what most people do, so the lines are really long. In the afternoon, you might have a better chance to get in quicker.

• You can have a cheap lunch inside the Vatican Museums. The price is much lower than the restaurants in the area around the Vatican. You can get a full lunch, but they also sell sandwiches and slices of Pizza.

• You can take pictures anywhere inside the museums, except the Sistine Chapel.

• Beware of pickpockets inside the Museums and especially inside the Sistine Chapel. On normal days it is really busy and everybody is looking up at the ceiling, so some pickpockets take advantage.

ABOUT THE AUTHOR

Paul den Arend grew up in the Netherlands and has been travelling for most of his adult life. He studied art history in Salamanca, Spain, wrote reports for the Dutch Embassy in Santiago de Chile and studied Chinese in China. In between, he has been working as a tour guide. For many years he lived in Rome, Italy and guided groups of all backgrounds through the city. He has been a guide in the Vatican Museums, Saint Peter's and the Galleria Borghese, but he also loves to show groups around Sicily or Tuscany. His guidebooks reflect a profound love for the Eternal City and the many stories about its beautiful piazza's and landmarks.

www.ingramcontent.com/pod-product-compliance
Lightning Source LLC
Chambersburg PA
CBHW071005180526
45168CB00003B/1294